Contents

Introduction

Magic is the art of doing tricks that defy the laws of nature. Magic is a great hobby and will let you amaze and entertain your family and friends. The tricks in *Magic with Cards* are fun and most of them are done with just an ordinary pack of cards. If you need to make extra props, there are clear instructions on how to do so.

How to learn tricks

1. Read through the whole trick twice. Don't worry if you do not understand everything at this stage.

2. Gather all the things you need.

3. Go through the trick again, doing the actions step by step.

4. If you are not comfortable with a particular action, see if you can adapt it to suit you better.

5. Now practise the various movements, making sure that your hands are in the right place and that you can move smoothly from one step to another.

6. Once you have practised the moves, you can start rehearsing the trick (performing it as if for a real audience).

7. When you are happy that you can perform the trick perfectly, try it out on your friends.

DID YOU KNOW...

... that you can find lots of interesting facts about the props you use in these circles ?

Top Tip

Watch out for this symbol to read some top tips! They will help you make more of a trick or give you useful extra information.

Magicians and their magic
In boxes like this one, you will find information about famous magicians and their tricks.

IT'S **mAGIc**

I WANT TO DO MAGIC

Magic
with Cards

Peter Eldin

Franklin Watts
London . Sydney

© Aladdin Books Ltd 2002
Produced by
Aladdin Books Ltd
28 Percy Street
London W1T 2BZ

ISBN 0–7496–4469–9

First published in Great Britain in 2002 by
Franklin Watts
96 Leonard Street
London EC2A 4XD

Designers:
Flick, Book Design & Graphics
Pete Bennett

Editor:
Leen De Ridder

Picture researcher:
Brian Hunter Smart

Illustrators:
Catherine Ward, Peter Wilks – SGA
Tony Kenyon – BL Kearley

Printed in UAE

A CIP catalogue record for this book is available
from the British Library.

Picture Credits:
abbreviations: l-left, r-right, b-bottom,
t-top, c-centre, m-middle
All photos by Select Pictures, except for:
19br – Bettmann/CORBIS.

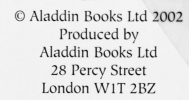

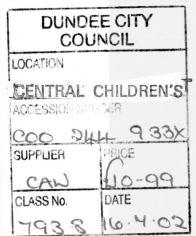

HINTS

• Never repeat a trick in the same company. The first showing of a trick amazes the audience. Do it again and they will know what is coming. The element of surprise will have gone and the trick will not go down so well. Because they know what is coming the second time round, it is also easier for the audience to work out how the trick is done.

• Your success as a magician will depend a lot on the way you present a trick. Even the simplest trick can look fantastic if you perform it confidently and without hesitating. This may sound like a strange piece of advice, but your performance of magic will improve if you believe that what you are doing really is magic. Believe you are doing real magic and you will be!

• When people ask how your tricks are done, do not tell them. Although many people may ask, they will be disappointed when you let them know how simple some tricks really are. Keep the secrets secret!

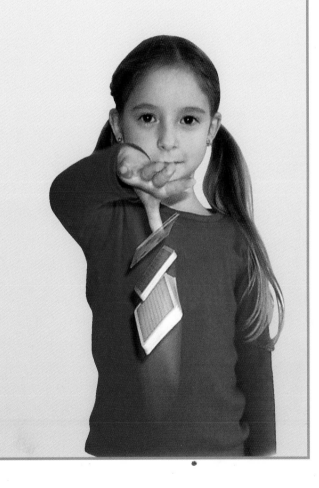

For some tricks you will need to cut the cards, which means removing a portion from the top of the pack. Some trick instructions will tell you to cut the cards and complete the cut. This means taking some cards from the top of the pack and placing them on the bottom of the pack.

Overhand shuffle

THE TRICK

Although it is not really a trick, the overhand shuffle is the most commonly used shuffle by magicians and card players. It is a very good way to mix your cards.

Preparation

> You will need:
> • a pack of cards

No preparation is needed – this is not a trick.

Top Tip

The smaller the packets you draw off with your left thumb, the better the shuffle will be and the more the cards will be mixed. If for any reason you do not want to mix the cards up too much, just pull off larger packets.

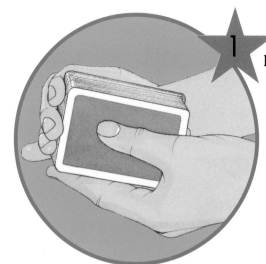

1 Hold the pack in your left hand with the cards resting on your fingers. Now pick up the cards using your right hand. Your thumb is at the nearest end and your first three fingers at the other end.

Lift the pack upwards and use your left thumb to pull some cards from the top of the pack and into the left hand. Bring your right hand back down so that your left thumb can draw off a few more cards.

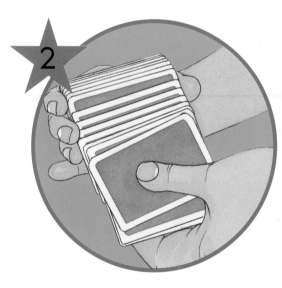

2

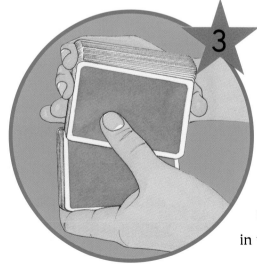

3 Lift your right hand once again and let the drawn-off cards fall on top of those already in your left hand. Keep drawing cards off in this way until the whole pack is back in your left hand.

False shuffle

1 Start an overhand shuffle as described on page 6, but instead of drawing off a packet of cards with the left thumb, pull off only one card (the top card in the pack). Shuffle the rest of the cards, drawing off packets in the normal way. When all the cards have been shuffled, the top card will be on the bottom of the pack.

2 Do another overhand shuffle, but work it so that just one card remains in the right hand. Draw off this final card onto the top of the pack to finish the shuffle. It looks as if you have done a completely fair shuffle but, without the spectators realising it, the bottom card is now on the top of the pack.

Top Tip

If you want to bring the bottom card to the top of the pack, just do step 2. It is a good idea to learn these shuffles well, because they can make a lot of card tricks more impressive.

Telling cut

THE TRICK

Shuffle a pack of cards, then ask a spectator to cut the pack anywhere he likes. Now use your magical powers to tell your impressed spectators what the top card of the other pile is!

Preparation

> **You will need:**
> • a pack of cards

1 Make sure you have practised the false shuffle on page 7, because you will need to use it in this trick.

2 Take a glimpse at the card on the bottom of the pack, and remember this card.

Shuffle the pack, secretly bringing the bottom card to the top as described in step 2 on page 7. Put the pack on your left palm, near to the wrist.

Ask a spectator to cut the cards anywhere he likes and to place the cut-off portion on the fingers of your left hand.

Fabulous fans

Richard Pitchford (1896-1973) performed with cigarettes and billiard balls but it was his skill with cards that gave him his stage name, Cardini. Throughout his act, fans of cards appeared unexpectedly from nowhere. As soon as he discarded one fan another would appear, astonishing him as much as the audience!

IT'S **mAGIc**

8

3

Now look at the card cut to (the top card of the pile near your wrist) and remember it. Say that this card will help you to work out what the top card of the other pile is. Pretend to think very hard for a moment, then name the top card of the other pile. (You know what this is because you looked at it and then shuffled it to the top.) Ask a spectator to check if you are right. And of course you are!

Top Tip

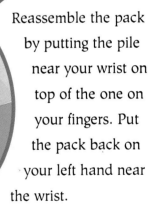

One of the rules of performing magic is that you should never repeat a trick in the same company. This trick is an exception to the rule. It should be done more than once to make it more effective and impressive. Do not do it more than three times, however, or your audience may start to work out what you are doing.

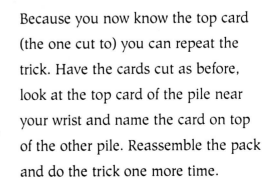

4

Reassemble the pack by putting the pile near your wrist on top of the one on your fingers. Put the pack back on your left hand near the wrist.

5

Because you now know the top card (the one cut to) you can repeat the trick. Have the cards cut as before, look at the top card of the pile near your wrist and name the card on top of the other pile. Reassemble the pack and do the trick one more time.

Friendly kings

In this astonishing trick, three Kings are distributed through the pack. Make them come together by just cutting the pack a few times...

Preparation

You will need:
• a pack of cards

Before you start, put all four Kings on the top of the pack.

1 Take three of the Kings from the top of the pack and show them to the audience.

2 Place one of them on the top of the pack, put one on the bottom of the pack. Push the third into the middle of the pack.

3 Cut the cards and complete the cut. The top and bottom Kings are now next to each other, together with the one that was on the top of the pack before, but which you didn't show the audience. Cut a few more times if you wish.

4 Now say that you will cast a spell over the pack and make the three Kings come together. Spread out the cards face up and there, sure enough, you will find three Kings together!

How odd

THE TRICK

A spectator chooses a card, puts it anywhere he likes in the pack, and you are able to find it!

Preparation

> You will need:
> • a pack of cards

1 Beforehand, go through the pack and put all the even numbered cards – twos, fours, sixes, eights, tens and Queens – in one pile. The rest of the cards will contain all the odd numbered cards – the aces, threes, fives, sevens, nines, Jacks and Kings.

2 Put the two piles of cards together with a Joker between them, as shown in the picture on the left.

3 Put the pack back in its box.

Take the pack from its box and spread just the centre portion of the cards in front of you.

Cut the cards at the Joker and put the two piles on the table. Ask someone to take any card from one half of the pack, look at it, remember it, then place it anywhere in the other half.

Put the cards back together. Now run the cards from hand to hand, with their faces towards you, and take out one card. This will be the very card the spectator chose! It is a simple matter to find the card: it will be the only even one among the odd cards, or the only odd one among the even cards.

Tricky twins

THE TRICK

A spectator and you each take a card from the pack and place it into the other's pocket without showing it. When you both take the card from your pocket, magically they turn out to be the same value and colour! Is it just luck, or have your special powers something to do with it?

Preparation

> You will need:
> • a pack of cards

Prepare for this trick by putting one card in your pocket. This can be any card you like, but in this trick, we will assume that it is the Eight of Clubs.

1 Shuffle the cards and ask a spectator to take any card from the pack and – without looking at it – hand it face down to you.

2 Place the card straight into your pocket along with the card you put there earlier (in our example, the Eight of Clubs). Make sure you know if you put this card behind or in front of the one you put there earlier. You need to know so that you can take out the right card at the end of the trick.

3 Now take the cards, look at them and remove one. Hand it to the spectator who has to put it, unseen, into his pocket. You actually take the matching card to the one you put in your pocket earlier (for our example, this would be the Eight of Spades).

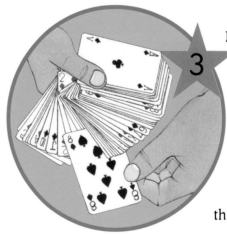

A cascade of cards

A Polish magician called Albini (1860-1913), always opened a new pack of cards when he did a card trick. This way he wanted to show the audience that he had not tampered with the cards before the show. It also meant that by the end of his performance, the stage was almost covered with discarded cards.

IT'S **MAGIC**

4

Ask the spectator to take the card from his pocket and show it to the audience.

Top Tip

If you go through the cards and cannot find the matching card to the one you secretly put in your pocket earlier, it means that the spectator has taken that card out. This means that you have a matching pair in your pocket. Make the most of this by saying that you put a card in your pocket before the show and get a spectator to remove the two cards to show the amazing coincidence. As a magician you sometimes need to improvise if everything does not go according to plan. Try and think before you perform your trick of what can go wrong and how you can react to it.

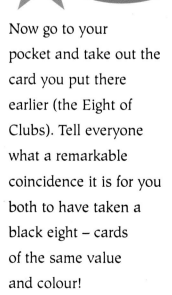

5

Now go to your pocket and take out the card you put there earlier (the Eight of Clubs). Tell everyone what a remarkable coincidence it is for you both to have taken a black eight – cards of the same value and colour!

Getting to the top

THE TRICK

Amaze your audience by making a card they chose appear miraculously on the top of the pack, even after you cut the cards. You can use this trick as a part of many other ones, but it is also suitable to do on its own.

Preparation

You will need:
• a pack of cards

Before you start, put the Joker on the bottom of the pack.

Spread out the cards and ask someone to pick any one, look at it and then replace it on the top of the pack. Cut the cards and complete the cut.

The chosen card is now next to the Joker somewhere in the pack. You can cut the cards a few more times if you like, because cutting the cards does not move the Joker away from the chosen card. Say that you have to remove the Joker for this trick, look through the pack and find the Joker.

DID YOU KNOW...

... that 'bicycles' are cards? This refers to the back design of cards made by The US Playing Card Co of Cincinnati. These cards are very popular with magicians and can be bought at most magic shops.

Cut the cards so that the Joker is on the bottom, and complete the cut. The chosen card is now on the top of the pack. With some dramatic movements remove the Joker and put it next to the pile of cards. Look at it as if it is telling you what the chosen card is.

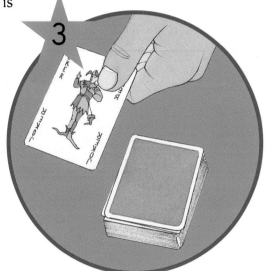

Cardicians

Some magicians who specialise in card magic call themselves 'cardicians'. This name comes from the title of a book by magician Ed Marlo (1913-1991). Marlo specialised in sleight-of-hand magic with cards and wrote several books on card magic. Many of his tricks are only performed by expert magicians, because they are very complicated and need lots and lots of practice!

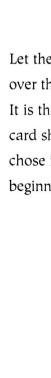

Let the spectator turn over the top card. It is the very card she chose in the beginning!

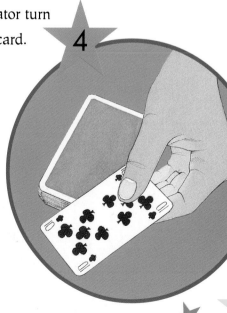

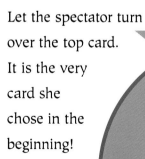

15

Going up

THE TRICK

In this great trick a spectator chooses a card and puts it anywhere in the pack. You not only find the card, but you also make it rise up from the pack!

Preparation

> **You will need:**
> • a pack of cards in its box
> • scissors

Prepare for this trick by cutting a slit out of the back of the card box, as shown in the picture below.

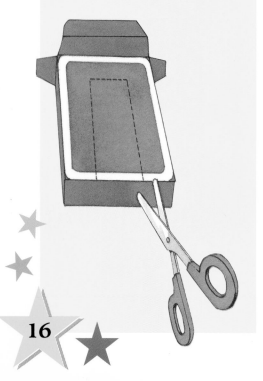

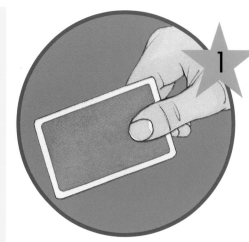

Ask someone from the audience to choose a card, remember it and show it to the audience.

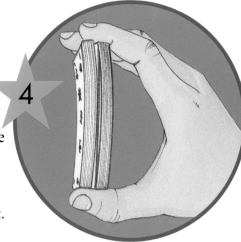

While the card is being shown, secretly bend all the cards in your hand.

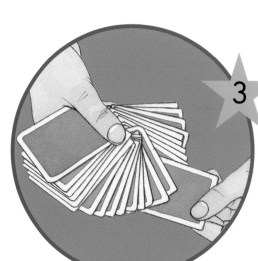

Ask the spectator to push his chosen card anywhere in the pack. Shuffle the cards.

If you look at the long edge of the pack, you will see a definite break in the cards at the chosen card. It can be seen because the chosen card is straight and all the rest are bent.

16

Now cut the cards at the break and put the top half of the pack to the bottom, so that the chosen card is now on top of the pack.

Top Tip

If you want to do another trick with the same pack of cards, just bend them back and they will be straight again and ready to use.

Put the cards in the card box with their faces towards the spectators. Do not close the box and be careful to keep the cut-out hidden from the audience.

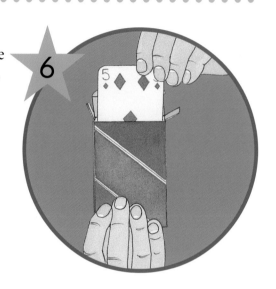

Ask the spectator to name the card she chose. The chosen card now seems to rise mysteriously from the pack...
It is, in fact, being pushed up by your thumb at the back of the box.

17

Turnover card

THE TRICK

A spectator chooses a card and puts it back somewhere in the pack. You drop the cards onto the table and – to everyone's amazement – the chosen card reveals itself by turning over in mid-air.

Preparation

> **You will need:**
> • a pack of cards

You will need to know one of the two tricks on pages 14-15 or 16-17. Steps 1 to 3 on pages 14-15 tell you how to bring a card to the top by using the Joker. On pages 16-17 you bend cards to find a chosen card and bring it to the top. See which of the two methods you like best to use in this trick.

1

Have a card chosen and returned to the pack. Bring it to the top of the pack using the method you prefer.

2

Hold the pack in your right hand with your thumb at one short end and your fingers at the other end.

Bring your hands together and use your left thumb to push the top (chosen) card to the right so that it overlaps the edge of the pack by about one centimetre. This projecting edge is hidden by the palm of your right hand.

3

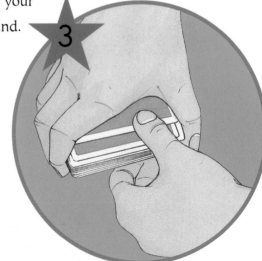

DID YOU KNOW...

...that there are 52 cards in a pack and there are 52 weeks in a year? The pack is divided into four suits and there are four seasons. Each suit contains 13 cards and there are 13 weeks in a season.

Hold the pack about 50 centimetres from the table top and drop it straight down.

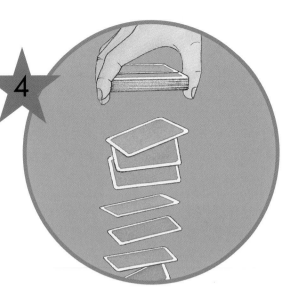

The upward rush of air causes the top card to turn over so that it ends up face up on the table!

IT'S mAGIc

Champion card thrower
Some performers have perfected the technique of throwing playing cards, or publicity cards, out into the audience. The American illusionist Howard Thurston (1869-1936) (below, right) was especially expert at this. The greatest card thrower today is Ricky Jay who is recorded as throwing a card an amazing distance of almost 60 metres!

19

Magnetic ribbon

THE TRICK

Someone chooses a card and returns it to the pack. You then bind the pack with a long ribbon and place it in a box. Lift one end of the ribbon and there, dangling from the other end, is the chosen card!

Preparation

> **You will need:**
> • a pack of cards
> • a ribbon (about 2.5 cm wide by 60 cm long)
> • a small piece of double-sided tape
> • a box

1 Stick the tape to one end of the ribbon.
2 You will need one of the two methods of bringing a card to the top of the pack described on pages 14-15 (steps 1 to 3) or pages 16-17 (steps 1 to 4).

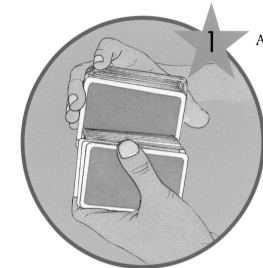

Ask a spectator to shuffle a pack of cards. Spread the cards out in front of him and ask him to take any card and show it to the audience.

The card is then returned to the pack. Secretly bring it to the top using whichever method you like best.

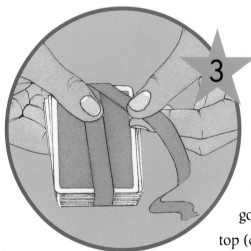

Pick up the taped end of the ribbon (keeping the tape hidden) and wrap the ribbon around the pack. Make sure that the tape goes against the back of the top (chosen) card.

If you do not have any double-sided tape, take a piece of ordinary tape and join the ends together to make a ring. Flatten out the ring of tape and it will do the job just as well.

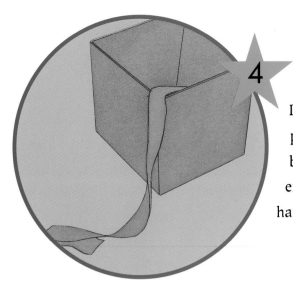

4

Put the wrapped pack into the box with the free end of ribbon hanging outside.

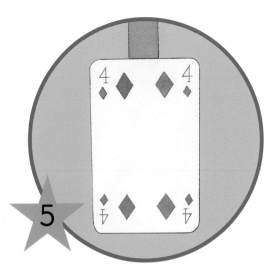

5

Ask for the name of the chosen card. Slowly and dramatically pull the ribbon from the box. There, stuck to the end of the ribbon, is the chosen card!

Top Tip

Once you know a couple of tricks, you can start combining them to make your own variations on tricks. To make more of the trick on this page, for example, you could do a false shuffle (see page 7) once the chosen card is on top of the pack. This will make the fact that you are able to find the card even more amazing. Use your imagination to mix tricks, or to make the ones you know more unique.

Royal weddings

THE TRICK

The four Kings and four Queens are mixed together, but you separate them into pairs of the same suit even though the cards are behind your back.

Preparation

You will need:
• the four Kings and four Queens from a pack of cards

1 Put the four Kings in one pile and the four Queens in another.
2 Make sure that the suits are in the same order in each pile (see above).
3 Put one pile on top of the other.

1 Spread the four Kings and four Queens out face up for the audience to see.

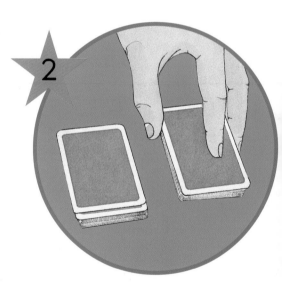

Close up the fan and cut the cards several times to give the impression that you cannot know the positions of any of the cards.

2

3 Put the cards behind your back and cut the cards so you have four cards in each hand.

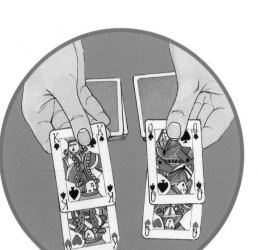

DID YOU KNOW...

...that playing cards probably originated in China or in Hindustan in about 800 AD? The four suits as we know them today originated in France in the 1500s.

4 Take the top card from each half and bring them forward. To everyone's amazement, they will be the King and Queen of the same suit. Keep taking pairs of cards until all of them have been produced, then take a bow.

Top Tip

Instead of taking the four Kings and Queens from the pack before doing this trick, you could put them in different parts of the pack. Then run through the cards and take out the Kings and Queens as they come into view. This is a much more natural way to start the trick. Provided you make sure that both sets of cards are in the same suit order beforehand, the trick will still work.

Surprise aces

THE TRICK

A spectator cuts the pack into four piles. You then move some cards around and, to everyone's astonishment, end up with an Ace on top of each of the four piles.

Preparation

You will need:
• a pack of cards

Before you begin, put the four Aces on top of the pack.

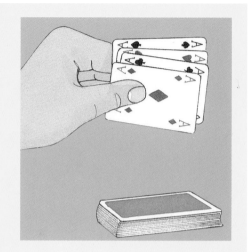

Put the cards on the table and ask a spectator to cut them into four piles. The piles do not have to be the same thickness, but once the cut has been made, it cannot be changed.

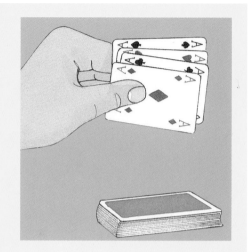

1

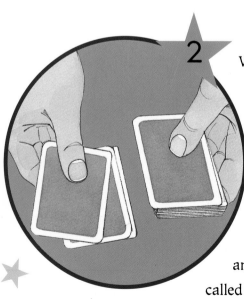

2

While the cutting is being done, keep track of which pile has the Aces on top. Now tell the audience you have to enact an ancient magic spell called 'Three under, three across'. Pick up one pile and transfer three cards from the top to the bottom of the pile.

24

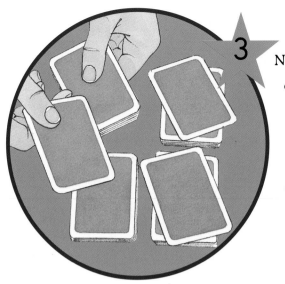

3 Now take three cards from the top of the pile and place one on top of each of the other three piles.

4 Do this with each pile in turn, but make sure that the pile with the Aces is the last pile you handle. (Because of the dealing you have done, this pile now has three cards on top of the four Aces.)

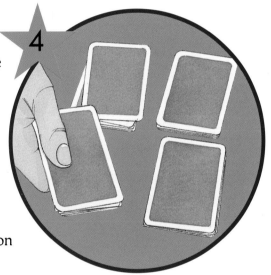

5 You now do the 'Three under, three across' with the last Aces pile. It seems that the cards have been well and truly mixed up, but when you ask a spectator to turn over the top card of each pile, she will find that they are all Aces!

IT'S **mAGIc**

Card beginners

A lot of magicians start with card tricks because playing cards are very easy to buy and there are literally thousands of tricks that can be done with them. Some magicians continue to specialise in card tricks (see 'Cardicians' on page 15), but most branch out into other types of magic.

• At the start of his career, the great Harry Houdini (1874-1926) performed as the 'King of Cards'. Only afterwards did he start developing the amazing escapes he is so famous for.

• It was a card trick, called 'The Rising Cards', that first made American magician Howard Thurston (see page 19) famous. He went on to become one of America's top illusionists, but he continued to perform 'The Rising Cards' in his shows.

Your card

THE TRICK

A spectator looks at the top card of one of five piles the pack is cut into. You simply reassemble them, let the magic force do its job, then name the card your spectator looked at.

Preparation

You will need:
• a pack of cards

Take a glimpse at the bottom card of the pack before you start. Remember this card.

1

Place the cards on the table and ask a spectator to cut them into five piles. Then ask him to look at the top card of any pile and remember it.

Gather up all the piles. It is important that the pile with the bottom card you remembered goes on top of the pile with the chosen card. The rest of the piles can be put back together in any order.

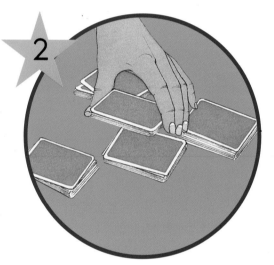

2

! If the spectator should look at the top card of the pile which has your memorised card, just ask him to cut the pile and complete the cut. He can then put the other piles together in any order he wishes.

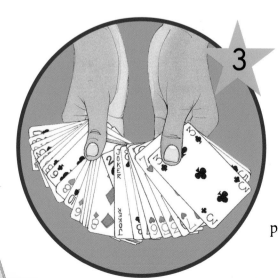

3

Whatever happens, the chosen card is now next to the card you have memorised. Run through the cards looking for your memorised card (the one originally on the bottom of the pack). The card before it will be the chosen card.

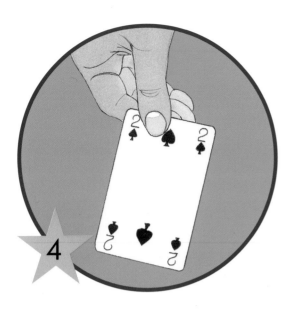

4

You can now simply put the card on the table to show you have found it or you can pretend to read the spectator's mind and tell him the name of the card he looked at.

Top Tips

• *To simplify and speed up this trick, you could use just three piles instead of five.*

• *The card you memorised in this trick is known to magicians as a 'key card'. It is the 'key' to helping you find the card a spectator chose. If you use your own pack of cards for this trick, you can make a different type of key card by putting a small ink mark on the back of one card (right).*

Make this mark as small as possible as you do not want anyone else to notice it. You have to secretly put your key card on the bottom of the pack before the show. Do the trick in the same way as described here, but this time, you do not have to look at the faces to find the chosen card. You can just spread the cards out face down and look for your secret mark. The card next to your key card will be the one the spectator chose.

Push this card forward and ask the spectator for the name of the chosen card. Then slowly and dramatically turn over the card on the table. It is the very same card!

Use your imagination to make the ending of the trick more or less spectacular, according to your style, but always remember to believe in what you are doing.

Numbered thoughts

THE TRICK

Randomly deal some cards onto the table. A spectator notes one of these cards and what position it is in. After cutting the cards a couple of times, simply ask her what position it was, and you will tell her what her card was!

Preparation

You will need:
• a pack of cards

Take about 15 cards and deal them, one by one, face up on the table. Memorise the first card dealt. Ask a spectator to remember one of the cards and at what number it is in the packet.

When the cards have been dealt, take a few more cards from the pack and add them to the ones on the table, so that the audience does not think you are using any mathematical method. Gather them up without disturbing the order and put them face down on the table.

Cut the cards and complete the cut. Do this several times to give the impression that all the cards are well mixed (but do not shuffle the cards).

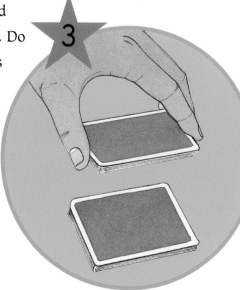

28

Ask the spectator at what number her card was when the cards were first dealt. Look through the cards and find the card you remembered at the beginning (the first card dealt). Start counting from that card until you reach the number the spectator has told you, and that will be the card he is thinking of.

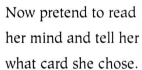

If you come to the end of the packet when counting the cards, simply carry on counting from the top.

Now pretend to read her mind and tell her what card she chose.

Top Tip

Once you are confident doing this trick, you can add extra parts to it. You can combine it with other tricks from this book or let your imagination run free and come up with an idea yourself. This of course goes for all tricks. However, when you start experimenting, there are some things to keep in mind.

Firstly, make sure your trick does not become too long. If the audience have to wait, they may lose interest or forget what the beginning of the trick was. Try to judge what the ideal length of a trick is.

Secondly, if you take parts of other tricks to add to this one, avoid doing the added trick before the same audience. They will recognise it, and they may start to work out how the trick works.

Card box

THE TRICK

Look into the future and predict what card a spectator will choose...

You will need:
- a box, large enough to take a pack of cards, with a hinged lid
- a piece of card
- a piece of paper
- a pen
- a pack of cards
- a pair of scissors

Preparation

1 Cut the piece of card so that it fits exactly into the lid and base of the box.

2 Paint the card the same colour as the interior of the box (card boxes sold by magic dealers are usually black inside). The card becomes a flap that rests either in the lid or the base, but which cannot be seen.

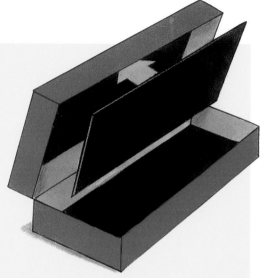

3 Remove the Eight of Hearts from the pack and put it in the lid of the box with the face of the card uppermost.

4 Put the flap over the card and leave the box open on your table.

You will choose the Eight of Hearts.

★ **1**

On the piece of paper write 'You will choose the Eight of Hearts'. Fold the paper and place it on your table.

Have the pack of cards shuffled. Ask a spectator to take any card and place it in the box without looking at it.

★ **2**

★ **3**

Now close the box. In that instant you have changed the chosen card for the card you placed in the box earlier, because as soon as you close the box the flap drops down.

Ask the spectator if she had a perfectly free choice of card. She did, so she will say yes. Then say: "Then isn't it amazing that I knew in advance what card you would choose?" Ask her to read the paper and take out the card. She reads the paper and takes out the card. You were absolutely right!

Top Tip

This card box can be used for lots of different tricks. Here are some ideas you can try. Work out how they are done using the box and then see if you can come up with some ideas of your own as well.

• Two spectators each choose a card from two different packs. The cards are placed, unseen, into the box. When the box is opened it is shown that both spectators chose exactly the same card.

• Several letter cards are chosen and dropped into the box. When they are taken out they spell the name of the spectator (which you will have to know in advance, of course).

• A playing card is chosen and torn into pieces which are dropped into the box. A few magic words, and when the box is opened the card is whole once more.

• A piece of plain paper is placed in the box. The lid is closed just for a second then the magician remembers he intended to put a pencil in the box as well. The box is closed again and when reopened there is spooky writing on the paper.

Index

Glossary of magic words

Break
An unseen gap in a pack of cards.
Fan
Spreading a pack of cards out into a fan shape.
Glimpse
To secretly look at a card.
Key card
A card that helps the magician find another card. It can be marked or memorised beforehand.

Prearranged pack
A pack of cards arranged in a particular order.
Set-up
The way props are arranged or a secret arrangement of playing cards for a trick.
Sleight-of-hand
A number of techniques where the magician's slick hand movements are used to manipulate objects and deceive the audience.

Websites and clubs

Have you caught the magic bug and want to know more? Here are some magic websites and addresses of clubs you could join:

•www.repromagic.co.uk
A list of clubs across the British Isles.

Magic tricks can be bought from:
•www.merlinswakefield.co.uk
•www.internationalmagic.com
•www.magictricks.com

• www.themagiccircle.co.uk
Site of the famous Magic Circle. Includes a virtual tour of some the club headquarters. The Magic Circle has a junior club:
Young Magicians' Club
Centre for the Magic Arts
12 Stephenson Way
London NW1 2HD
www.youngmagiciansclub.co.uk

•www.pauldaniels.co.uk – Biography and pictures of Britain's most famous magician.